Music Matters

FOLK MUSIC
in Britain, Ireland and the USA

Clive D. Griffin

Dryad Press Limited   London

Typeset by Tek-Art Ltd, Kent
and printed and bound by
Anchor Press Ltd
Tiptree, Essex
for the Publishers,
Dryad Press Limited,
4 Fitzhardinge Street,
London W1H 0AH

ISBN 0 8521 9795 0

ACKNOWLEDGMENTS

Special thanks go to Keith Griffin of the Welsh
Amateur Music Federation.

The Author and Publishers thank the following
for their kind permission to reproduce
copyright illustrations: BBC Hulton Picture
Library, pages 1, 8, 12, 25, 27, 28, 29, 32, 35,
36, 38, 39, 40-1, 43 (The Bettmann Archive), 44
(The Bettmann Archive); Keystone Collection,
pages 10, 20-1, 23, 24, 42, 45, 46-7, 48, 49, 50-
1, 52, 53, 54-5; National Museum of Wales,
Welsh Folk Museum, pages 7, 14, 15, 17. The
maps on pages 59 and 60 were drawn by R.F.
Brien.

The cover photograph of The Chieftains is
reproduced courtesy of Photo Images, Dublin.

CONTENTS

PART ONE

WHAT IS FOLK MUSIC?

At the beginning of the nineteenth century, the answer to this question would have been easy. Folk, as the name implies, was the music of the people, the vast majority of whom worked on the land. Folk music was their entertainment, a means of making work seem lighter and an accompaniment to the ancient rituals still performed at various times of the year. Musicians were amateurs, who performed for their fellow workers, friends and neighbours. The word "amateur" is not used in any derogatory sense, as it sometimes is today. Traditional musicians were highly respected within their communities. This attitude is voiced by one of the characters in Thomas Hardy's novel *Return of the Native*. (Although Hardy's characters were fictitious, they were based on close observation of real people.)

"Whenever a club walked he'd play the clarinet in the band that marched before 'em as if he'd never touched anything but a clarinet all his life. And then, when they got to church door he'd throw down the clarinet, snatch up the bass viol, and rozum away as if he'd never played anything but a bass viol. Folk would say – folk that know'd what a true stave was – 'Surely that's never the same man that I saw handling the clarinet so masterly by now'."

Traditional musicians were not merely keeping alive an unchanging body of songs and dances. They were happy to absorb themes and ideas from other sources, including the street ballads which were produced in the towns. Printers would pay ballad writers to recount noteworthy current events in verse form. The resultant songs were printed on sheets of paper and sold in the streets. They were cheaper than newspapers and could be more imaginative in their interpretation of the facts.

The nineteenth century, however, was a period of great change. The growth of the industrial towns and the movement away from the countryside upset the old order. Professional entertainers challenged the role of traditional musicians. At the same time, there was a growing interest in folk music amongst the middle classes. This was partly a result of the new mood of nationalism which was sweeping through Europe. Many composers were anxious to give their music a national flavour and borrowed tunes from the folk music of their countries. There was also a genuine interest in collecting folk-songs for their own sake. The English composer, RALPH VAUGHAN WILLIAMS (1872-1958), used themes from English folk music in his work and also collected folk-songs.

Middle-class folk-song collectors were not always welcomed by the singers themselves. Kitty Idwal Jones tells the story of one who was rebuffed:

"A warning to the would-be collector was the story of Hannah Sheeptrotters.

Thomas Hardy: *(1840-1928). English poet and novelist. His novels are all set in Wessex, an area in the south-west of England.*

Kitty Idwal Jones: *the daughter of Lady Herbert Lewis, who was a keen folk-song collector and president of the Welsh Folk-Song Society from 1930-46.*

Hannah was an old woman who used to sell sheep's trotters around Holywell before ending up in the infirmary. She had a wealth of songs at her command but only sang to people she liked. One day the vicar brought a "county" lady to hear some of her songs. Hannah found the lady patronising, and refused to sing. Finally, after much pressure from the vicar, Hannah did sing – the most scurrilous song she knew. Hasty exit of vicar and lady! 'She won't come again,' remarked Hannah with great satisfaction."
("Adventures in Welsh Folk-Song Collecting", *Welsh Music*, Vol. 5, No. 5 spring 1987)

The best-known collector in England was CECIL SHARP, who died in 1924. Such collectors felt that they first had to define exactly what it was that they were collecting. Unfortunately, many of their definitions of folk music were rather limiting. Sharp, for example, said that folk-songs were "to be found only in those country districts which, by reason of their remoteness, have escaped the infection of modern ideas." Another collector, ALFRED WILLIAMS, concluded that the collector's task was to preserve folk-songs before they disappeared for ever. "We live in a new age, almost in a new world. Life has changed. There are other amusements. We move at a quicker pace . . . . Let us, then, be content to say that folk-song is dead" (*Folk-Songs of the Upper Thames*, 1923).

Collectors often allowed their own middle-class values to cloud their judgement. Songs were "tidied up" and given new musical accompaniments, while words which might give offence to delicate ears were removed. Worst of all, there was a rather romantic idea of what constituted a "traditional" song. Sharp spoke of folk-singers as being "the last of a long line that stretches back into the mists of far-off days" and rejected those items in a singer's repertoire which he regarded as

modern additions. The problem with this attitude, of course, is that all songs were modern at some time and there have always been additions to the body of songs that constitutes folk music.

Later collectors adopted a less restrictive attitude. PERCY GRAINGER (1882-1961), for example, was interested in the way that performers interpreted songs. He advocated the use of recording equipment – very bulky and primitive in his day – rather than pencil and paper for capturing songs. He also tried to develop a method of notating songs exactly as they were sung, rather than trying to fit them into conventional musical notation. It was not until the 1950s, though, that any serious interest was shown in collecting folk-songs from the industrial areas. A.L. Lloyd and Ewan MacColl found that there was a vast source of music, largely unknown outside the communities in which it was sung.

With the "folk revival" of the 1960s, definitions of folk music often became so wide-reaching as to be meaningless. For the major record companies, any singer-songwriter with an acoustic guitar was a folk-singer. (In fact, the guitar was a late arrival so far as folk music is concerned. Earlier songs were accompanied by fife and tabor, fiddles and concertinas, while there are still purists who would argue that "true" folk music is always sung unaccompanied.) There is a need to distinguish between folk music and music which is performed in what is popularly regarded as a folk style. It is important to look at the *reason* for singing rather than the style of music. Folk music is the music of a community, made by members of that community primarily for other members.

---

notation: *a system of recording music on paper, using written symbols.*

---

fife and tabor: *a combination of a three-holed flute and a small drum, generally played by one musician. Used in many forms of dance music in the Middle Ages.*

The development of modern recording techniques allowed the music of traditional singers to reach a much wider audience.

Traditionally this community would have been defined by a geographical location or a shared occupation. In the twentieth century, however, it could be argued that there is also a third kind of community – that of people united by a common political or social aim. Folk musicians are aware of the traditions of their community and draw upon them in their songs. They might receive financial reward for their music, but this is not their main aim. The great American folk-singer, WOODY GUTHRIE, wrote at the bottom of the page in one of his collections of songs that "the above song was written by Woody Guthrie and legally deposited at Washington DC, under copyright number 75623489108663. Anyone discovered singing it without my prior permission will certainly be a good friend of mine, because that's what I wrote it for."

PART TWO

THE CELTS

The English are relative newcomers to the British Isles. The influence of the earlier inhabitants of these islands, the Celts, survives in Ireland, Scotland and Wales. Archeologists believe that the Celtic tribes originated in what are now parts of Hungary and Austria. It was here that the knowledge of iron-working was introduced to Europe and a new tribal aristocracy developed, uniting the warring tribes of the area and spreading their own language and culture. They swept across north-western Europe, reaching the British Isles about 2000 years ago. They arrived not as

a huge invading army, but in small tribal groups which absorbed rather than eliminated the original inhabitants. Their languages can be divided into two groups – *Goidelic* (Gaelic) and *Brythonic* (British), the ancestor of modern Welsh.

The Celts were a warlike people. "The whole race is madly fond of war, high-spirited and quick to battle", wrote one Roman commentator. They also loved music and poetry, however. When the Anglo-Saxons began settling in what is now England, about 1500 years ago, the Celts were pushed gradually westwards. The Norman invasion of 1066 caused the decline in Celtic power to continue throughout the British Isles. Norman barons seized land, first in Wales, then in Ireland and Scotland. There were uprisings and rebellions, but gradually English control increased. Landlords living in England owned vast estates in Ireland, Scotland and Wales which they never visited. They cared about the profits from these estates, not the people living on them. Although the Celts lost political power, however, their culture survived. It was kept alive by the ordinary people, as their former rulers had largely adopted English speech and customs. Speaking a Celtic tongue was a handicap to those who wished to make their way in the world. What was once an aristocratic culture thus became a folk one. Celtic culture did not survive unchanged, of course, but the folk music of Ireland, Scotland and Wales is markedly different from that of England. The following pages offer a brief introduction to the subject.

Bards, like the one pictured on the left, were Celtic poet/musicians. Celtic chieftains and princes all maintained bards to sing their praises and keep alive the history of their people. During the Middle Ages, the English tried to destroy the bardic tradition, seeing it as a focus for rebellion. Many bards became wandering musicians.

The Celtic harp is much smaller than the Italian instrument used in orchestras, and has a curved column joining the top to the base.

Ireland

At the root of Irish folk music is a singing style known as *sean nós* (old style). It is a complex style, highly ornamented, and unaccompanied.

"In the small rural communities in which it developed, the *sean nós* was very much more than mere entertainment. It contained among its large repertoire the religious songs of a people who were not allowed the luxury of public devotion, their work songs and songs of love, their humorous songs and the stories of local tragedies . . . . Here too were the thinly disguised songs of rebellion, the glorification of past heroes coupled with a message of hope for a new awakening . . . [and] simple local happenings, perhaps adding a new dimension of fantasy to the event to provide the heroic element so necessary for an oppressed people." (Tomás Ó Canainn, *Traditional Music in Ireland*)

Along the west coast, in the areas where Irish is still spoken today (the *Gaeltacht*), songs of shipwreck are common. The following lines show something of the power of such songs, even in translation.

"The sea roared and the strong waves lashed
The clouds gathered and the mist came down.
If the boat planks could speak what a story they'd tell
Of the nearness of death and how they saved us all.
My hands are torn from pulling ropes,
The skin and flesh are hauled out of the bone
But if the Son of God has promised us death
What's the point of going against Him,
Let's all go to Heaven together now."
"*Caiptín Ó Máille*"(Captain O'Malley)

The area of the west coast of Ireland where Irish is still spoken is known as the Gaeltacht.

Other songs tell of heroes, many of whom went to fight abroad, and small local skirmishes are elevated into great battles. Not all soldiers are depicted heroically, however. "*An Saighdiúr Tréigthe*" ("The Deserted Soldier") is about one who deliberately wounds himself in order to avoid fighting.

Despite the influence of the Catholic Church, many love songs display a rather free attitude to marriage and whether sex should come before or after it. "*Slán agus beannacht le buaireahm an tsaoil*" ("early next morning we'll send for the priest"). In common with many other colonized countries, Ireland also has a strong tradition of "treason" songs. These have harmless choruses but preach sedition in their verses. When Ireland was ruled from London, English listeners with only a small knowledge of Irish would possibly understand the former, but not the true meaning of the latter.

Sean nós has had a strong influence on instrumental styles. Traditionally, instrumental music is performed by solo musicians. Melodies are fixed, but players are expected to add their own, often extremely elaborate, ornamentation to them. The bagpipes appeared in Ireland as early as the eleventh century. The Irish *uillean* pipes differ from the Scottish pipes in that air is supplied to the bag by a bellows operated by the player's arm. The tin whistle is another commonly used instrument, a descendant of earlier instruments made from bone. The style of playing is very much influenced by pipe music. The fiddle was introduced from Scotland in the sixteenth century. The manner of fiddle-playing varies throughout the country from the loud, driving music of Donegal to the softer, more ornate style of Sligo.

Although Irish folk music is essentially a solo form, in the 1920s small bands began to appear. Known as *ceilidh* bands, they consisted of eight or nine musicians playing in unison. They used fiddles and accordions and gradually the influence of American popular music began to creep in. To combat what he saw as this threat, the composer and teacher, SEAN Ó RIADA, formed *Ceoltoiri Chualann*, a group dedicated to playing traditional Irish music. Some of its members went on to form THE CHIEFTAINS, who have done much

to bring the music to a wider audience. The Chieftains have been followed by several other successful groups, among them THE DUBLINERS, PLANXTY and CLANNAD. The music of THE POGUES also draws heavily on Irish folk traditions while THE BOYS OF THE LOUGH mix folk music from Ireland, Scotland and the Isle of Man. Irish groups have had a great influence on folk musicians in both Scotland and Wales.

Scotland

Scottish folk music can be divided into that of the Highlands, where English influence was small, and that of the Lowlands, where it was more obvious. Until the sixteenth century, Highland clan chiefs employed bards to write songs and poems for various occasions. They also maintained pipers. In the eighteenth century, the English government attempted to suppress the pipes, along with other elements of Scottish culture, and they never regained their place in folk music. They did, however, become the main feature of Scottish military music. The attempted suppression of Scottish culture and the eviction of Highlanders from their lands was English revenge following the Jacobite rebellions of 1715 and 1745. These feature largely in Scottish folk music, together with more general complaints about the injustice of English rule. "MacPherson's Rant", for example, tells of a fiddler who is condemned to death. On the day of his execution, news reaches his captors that a reprieve is on its way. Their solution is to put the clocks forward so that he is hanged just as the messenger bearing the reprieve arrives.

---

unison: *two or more instruments playing the same tune without any harmony.*

Jacobite: *When James II abdicated in 1688, those who still followed him were known as Jacobites. His son, James ("The Old Pretender"), and his grandson, Charles ("The Young Pretender"), both laid claim to the English throne and had widespread support in Scotland. The Jacobite cause was finally lost at the Battle of Culloden.*

In 1746 Culloden Moor, near Inverness in Scotland, was the site of the last battle to be fought on British soil. The army of Prince Charles Edward Stuart ("The Young Pretender") was defeated by an English force led by the Duke of Cumberland.

Gaelic still survives in many areas of the Scottish Highlands and in the Western Isles it is the everyday language of much of the community. These islands have a rich musical tradition, though this is now threatened by outside influences. As in all Celtic music, poetry and melody are closely linked, with the rhythms of the language forming part of the music. The best-known songs are those which were sung to accompany different types of work, particularly the "waulking of cloth. This is a process which makes cloth heavier and more compact through shrinking and beating. It is group work, traditionally performed around a waulking board in the weaver's own home. The work was done by women, who also generally composed the songs. One woman would sing the verses alone, and the refrain would be sung by the whole group. Often the refrain consisted of meaningless words, chosen for their sound. A hard night's work would often be followed by a social gathering, with singing and dancing.

The "bothy ballads" were a product of north-eastern Scotland. A bothy was a stone outbuilding in which unmarried farm labourers were accommodated. During the nineteenth century, these labourers were hired at "feeing fairs". A man looking for employment wore a plait of straw in his buttonhole or pinned to the side of his bonnet. This was removed when he was hired. Conditions for these labourers were hard. The bothy would consist of two rooms, one in which the labourers ate their meals and the other in which they slept. Their food consisted mainly of "brose" — oatmeal and boiling water. Many came out in a rash, known as "Scotch fiddle", caused by this monotonous diet. The hours of work were long and, as there was no union to protect the men, victimization was common. "He [the foreman] pulled me oot ow'r the cairt and thrashed me wi' a back chain . . . . I was aboot 14 or 15 year auld at the time" (Jimmy MacBeath, later to become one of the best-known singers of bothy ballads). During the evening, these labourers would pass the time swapping songs, some of them traditional, others more modern. As labourers generally moved to a new farm once their six-month term was up, these songs were constantly being introduced to different audiences.

Many of the songs are about the physical conditions endured by farm labourers:

"At five o'clock we quickly rise
And hurry doon the stair;
It's there to corn our horses,
Likewise to straik their hair,
Syne, after working half an hour
Each to the kitchen goes,
It's there to get our breakfast,
Which generally is brose."

But there are also comic songs, songs of adventure and love songs. The last often describe the difficulties which the working classes faced in their courtship. A good deal of this romance had to be conducted at night, often in secret. The song "As I Cam Ower The Muir O Ord", for example, tells of a woman refusing to open the door to her lover in case her parents hear the hinges squeaking.

"My bedroom doors they chirp and cheep
So I cannae let ye in
Gang ye hame this ae night
An never come back again."

In this case, the woman is persuaded to oil the hinges "an the auld fowk heard nae din".

Farm labourers also entertained themselves with instrumental music. Bothy bands used instruments such as fiddles, mouth organs and tin whistles. The rhythm would be accentuated by the drumming of booted heels on the "cornkister" – the box which contained the horses' fodder. Dance tunes were also sung, using nonsense syllables. This was an art known as "diddling" or mouth music. It was common throughout Lowland Scotland and also found in Ireland and Wales. The high spot of the labourer's year was the "meal and ale", a feast to celebrate the bringing in of the harvest. The staple diet of oatmeal would be mixed with several bottles of whisky and followed by huge helpings of mutton broth. The evening ended with dancing – jigs, reels and strathspeys. The bothy system was harsh, but it kept a vast store of folk music alive well into the twentieth century.

Wales

In Wales, as in other Celtic countries, the division between music and poetry was blurred. The Welsh word *cerdd*, refers to both instrumental music (*cerdd dant*) and poetry (*cerdd dafod*). *Penillion* is a Welsh tradition which links poetry amd music. A harpist plays a well-known air, while a singer makes up poetry and sets it to an improvised tune which fits around the air which the harpist is playing. Sometimes the harp was replaced by a singer using nonsense syllables. This form of mouth music, *cerdd wefus*, was similar to the Scottish "diddling" mentioned earlier. *Penillion* has survived into the present century, though the importance of improvisation has declined and often the art consists only of putting together two different tunes, one sung, the other played.

In the Middle Ages Welsh musicians were famous for their playing of the *crwth*

---

improvise: *to make up as you go along.*

13

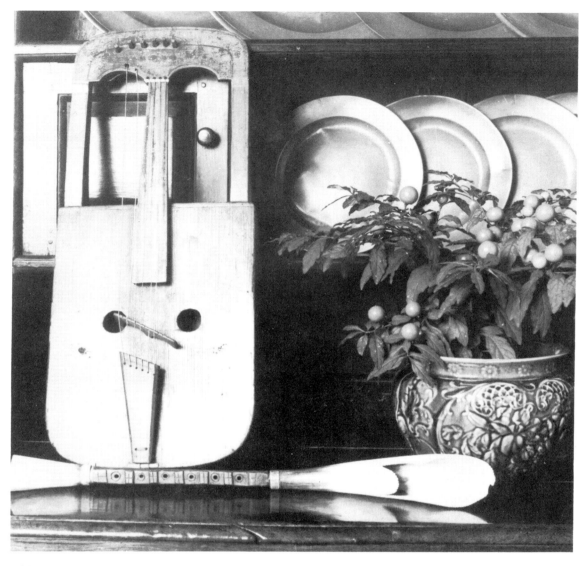

Although it is improvised, penillion *traditionally follows certain rules. For example, the voice must always begin after the harp but end with it.*

The crwth *and the* pibgorn, *two early Welsh instruments. The crwth was a bowed string instrument with five or six melody strings and a larger number which vibrated to provide a drone accompaniment. The pibgorn was a reed instrument consisting of a wooden pipe and a curved bell made from animal horn.*

and the harp. The Welsh "triple harp" had three sets of strings running parallel to each other, each set at a different pitch. Although this instrument was invented in Italy in the eighteenth century, it was in Wales that its possibilities were most fully developed. The bagpipes existed in Wales, as in other Celtic countries, but were never as popular as the harp and fell into disuse. Every great landowner had a

resident harpist and, after the Tudors ascended the English throne, many of

Tudors: *an English royal house descended from a Welshman, Owen Tudor. The first Tudor monarch, Henry VII, came to power in 1485.*

these became well-known in London. Their music became changed, however, to suit the tastes of an English audience. The Welsh tradition was an oral one, and had been supported by the patronage of land-owners. When these patrons began to look towards England for their culture, Welsh music was left in the care of the lower classes, who were almost all Welsh-speaking.

"There was poverty, even grinding poverty, a-plenty, but this was still a high-spirited peasantry, behaving with Bruegel-like boisterousness on feast-days, delighting in the ballad singers and in the interludes supplied by strolling players" (Wynford Vaughan-Thomas, *Wales: A History*, Michael Joseph, 1985). The folk-song "*Ambell i Gân*" ("Now And Again") tells how a song will keep the spirits high, turn darkness into light and make burdens seem easier. The last verse shows the importance of singing to the Welsh, when it says that in Heaven there will be singing always, not just now and again ("*Gobeithaf gael canu, nid ambell i gân*").

Wales had a folk tradition which was as vigorous as those of Ireland and Scotland, but it has not survived in as healthy a condition. There are three reasons for this. The first is, strangely enough, a late eighteenth-century desire to preserve Welsh culture. Unfortunately, the Welsh men and women – many of them living in London – who had this aim also had a tendency to muddle history and romantic legend. They wished to promote the idea of a Welsh nation and were quite happy to use myths and deliberate forgeries to do this. Many of today's popular ideas about "Welsh" culture stem from this period. The druids, for example, were ancient Celtic priests, but the modern ideas of the druids,

the *Gorsedd* circle, the bards in their robes and all the other trimmings of the National *Eisteddfod* came from the fertile imagination of Edward Williams, an eighteenth-century Glamorganshire stonemason, better known as Iolo Morganwg. In his passion for Welsh history, he happily forged manuscripts and poems, and these were seized upon by London Welsh societies such as the *Gwyneddogion*. The first meeting of the *Gorsedd* actually took place on Primrose Hill in London.

The two other threats to Welsh folk music were religious and economic. In the early eighteenth century a great religious revival began in Wales as the majority of the people turned away from the Church of England towards Nonconformist chapels. During the nineteenth century, the chapel became as important in Welsh culture as the Roman Catholic church in that of Ireland. This religious revival may have done much for hymn-singing in Wales, but it was disastrous as far as folk music was concerned. The chapel authorities frowned upon such music, which was dismissed as *canu maswedd* (ribald singing). Their purpose was to prepare people for the next world; the pleasures of this one were to be put aside.

At the same time as this religious revolution, Wales was feeling the impact of industrialization. In 1800, the Welsh population numbered less than half a million, the vast majority of whom were involved in agriculture. By 1914 the population had risen to over two million, more than 80 per cent of whom were living in towns. The main magnet was the coal-fields of South Wales. There was a massive movement of people from rural areas to the Rhondda Valley. A Cardiganshire folk-

---

Bruegel: *Pieter Bruegel (1525-69), a Flemish painter noted for his pictures of peasant life.*

Gorsedd: *a meeting of bards and druids.*

Eisteddfod: *historically, an Eisteddfod was a meeting where the status of bards was regulated through competitions. Bards were divided into three categories:* prydydd *(poet),* teuluwr *(family bard) and* clerwr *(wandering musician).*

16

Welsh social life in the nineteenth century was dominated by the influence of the chapel.

song of the period, "*Cân y Cardi*", tells of a young man boasting that he can earn far more as a coal-miner than his father could as a farm labourer. By the beginning of the twentieth century there were almost 16,000 such "Cardis" in Glamorgan. Another Cardiganshire song, "*Ar y Ffordd*

Cardi: *a native of Cardiganshire (now part of Dyfed).*

17

Wrth Fynd i Rymni" ("On The Way To Rhymney"), tells of a Cardiganshire lad's adventures on his way to the coal-field. These include a fight with nine Irishmen, a reference to the vast influx of non-Welsh workers into South Wales. By 1861, there were 18,000 Irish people living in South Wales, along with other workers from Devon and Somerset. By the beginning of this century, more than half the population of the coal-field had been born outside Wales.

The Welsh Folk-Song Society was founded in 1906. Its members dedicated themselves to collecting Welsh folk-songs before they disappeared completely. Like the slightly earlier collectors in England, they confined themselves to collecting in rural areas. It is a shame that the songs of the industrial towns were not recorded so carefully. The music heard in the public houses of a town like Merthyr Tydfil in its heyday must have been a heady mixture of different styles and traditions.

PART THREE

MEMORIES OF AN ANCIENT PAST

We like to think nowadays that we have control over nature. We can turn on an electric light when it gets dark, put on the central heating when it gets cold and watch our televisions to find out what is happening in other parts of the country. Occasionally, however, a snowstorm or a power-cut reminds us of what it must have been like during the long winter months for earlier inhabitants of these islands. It is hard to imagine how short the days must have seemed in December and how the first signs of spring must have caused such rejoicing. There were many ceremonies and rituals associated with different periods of the year. Some of these have survived to our own day, though their origins are generally forgotten. They are also celebrated in folk-song and dance.

These ceremonies were generally to do with making sure that the ground produced crops and animals were healthy. Long ago, animals such as the ram were worshipped as symbols of fertility. A number of folk-songs about rams of enormous size still survive today and are a distant echo of this animal worship. Among these are "The Derby Ram" and "The Exmoor Ram".

"The butcher who killed that ram
He was up to his neck in blood
And four and twenty butcher boys
Was washed away in the flood."
(From "The Derby Ram" collected by Ralph Vaughan Williams)

There were ancient dances in which people dressed in animal skins and green leaves. Holly and ivy were important symbols because they retained their greenery throughout the winter. Bonfires were lit in the middle of winter to represent the light of the sun, which appeared to be dying.

The battle between winter and spring was seen in terms of death and resurrection. Throughout northern Europe, there were myths about the king whose magical powers kept the land fertile. When this king died, the land was laid waste and became barren. When he came back to life, the land became fertile once more. Long ago, these myths were re-enacted through human sacrifices. Later, the sacrifices became symbolic. Figures made from plaited corn would be buried in the ground before the sowing of seeds. The figure of "John Barleycorn" is a common one in folk music, while nowadays "corn dollies" have become a rather trendy kitchen decoration. These old beliefs influenced the legends of King Arthur and Robin Hood, and form part of the rituals we still observe at Christmas and Easter. When Christianity came to the British Isles, the old traditions were not forgotten, but were incorporated into Christian festivals celebrated at the same times of the year.

Mid-winter

Ritual feasting and the lighting of bonfires are both far older than either Christmas or Guy Fawkes Night. The Romans held a week-long mid-winter festival, known as "Saturnalia". It was in honour of Saturn, the god of agriculture. This involved much eating, drinking and general merrymaking. In Norse mythology, this was the time when

---

Norse: *another name for the Vikings.*

the god Woden hurtled across the sky in his chariot, bearing gifts. Woden's place was eventually taken by a Christian saint whose feast day fell at a similar time – Saint Nicholas, or Santa Claus.

The May Day hobby-horse at Minehead in Somerset. The roots of this custom go back to the time when people dressed in animal skins for fertility ceremonies.

Most of the carols we now sing at Christmas were written during the nineteenth century, but carols actually have much older roots. The word comes from an old French word meaning "to dance", and carols were sung both at Christmas and in May. These old carols are very much concerned with looking forward to the spring and a hope for good crops.

"Bud and blossom, bud and blossom,
    bud and blossom bear,
So we may have plenty and cider all
    next year,
Hatfuls and in cupfuls and bushel bags
    and all,
And the cider running out of every gutter
    hole."

Such carols were sung when people went *wassailing*. This involved dancing and singing from village to village, often in fancy dress, asking for gifts in return for a song. The giving of gifts was meant to bring the donor good luck.

Another Christmas custom which was common in country districts well into the nineteenth century, and is still not totally dead today, was the *mumming* play. This was a dramatic portrayal of the contest

between darkness and light. There are certain traditional characters. The hero is represented by Saint George, the villain by the Turkish Knight. The Knight kills Saint George, but he is brought back to life by the Doctor. Father Christmas, often carrying a holly branch, acts as compere.

Springtime

Carols were also sung during May and, once again, this was a means for poor people to obtain charity.

"A branch of May it does look gay
As before your door I stand
It's naught but a sprout, but it's well
    budded out
By the work of God's own hand.

I have a bag within my hand,
'Tis drawn with a silken string,
And all I ask is a little silver
To line it well within."

Ralph Vaughan Williams told about one such singer:

"When Hoppy was young, he and his friends would go out each May Eve, singing all through the short darkness and being given drinks at each house they visited. As time went on, the singers became less enthusiastic, and finally only he and another elderly man kept up the custom. Hoppy's head was by then less good than it might have been, or, there being only two of them, they drank more at each call. On their way, he slipped and fell into a ditch, and his friend failed to pull him out of it. Not wishing to lose the money they were to be given as well as refreshment, the friend went on. Hoppy lay there listening to the May song, now near, now further away, as the dawn was breaking and his friend went singing from cottage to cottage till it was day."
(*Folk Songs Collected By Ralph Vaughan Williams*, edited by Roy Palmer, J.M. Dent, 1983)

Children dancing around the maypole at Combe (Oxfordshire) in 1953.

Perhaps the best known of all the spring customs is maypole dancing. Although we now tend to see it as an innocent English pastime, in previous centuries its pagan origins were more obvious.

"Against May, Whitsonday, or other time, all the young men and maides, olde men and wives, run gadding over night to the woods, groves, hills and mountains, where they spend all night in pleasant pastimes; and in the morning they return, bringing with them birch and branches of trees, to deck their assemblies withall . . . . But the chiefest jewel they bring from thence is their May-pole, which they bring home with great veneration . . . [it] is covered all over with floures and hearbs, bound round with strings, from the top to the bottome, and sometimes painted with variable coulours, with two or three hundred men, women and children following it with great devotion. And thus beeing reared up . . . then fall they to daunce about it."
(Philip Stubbs, *Anatomie of Abuses*, 1583)

Other elements of May Day celebrations were the election of a May Queen, sword dancing or morris dancing, a hobby-horse dance and a Robin Hood play. Robin Hood often represented the May King, while Maid Marian was the May Queen. There were echoes in this of the myth of the king whose power brings back the crops — often represented as the Green Man. The hobby-horse dance, which still survives in some parts of the country, features a man disguised in an animal costume. The sword dance is performed by men representing a medicine man and his six sons. The sons put the father to death, but

The Yorkshire Long Sword Dance being performed in the village of Goathland.

at the end of the dance he rises again. These are clearly remnants of the much older rituals just described.

Morris dancing has changed little since the fifteenth century. The origins of the word are not clear, but some people suggest it is a corruption of "Moorish". Similar dances are found in Brittany, which suggests that it has Celtic roots. One form of the dance which survived in North Wales was known as the "*Cadi Ha*". The dancers would black their faces and dress in women's clothes. The morris dancing most commonly seen nowadays originated in the Midlands. It involves six men wearing hats decorated with flowers, white shirts, knee breeches and cross-gartered stockings. Further north, in Lancashire, they wear clogs on their feet. The dancers are accompanied by the accordion or concertina and perform intricate movements using short sticks and white handkerchiefs. Traditionally, these dances were performed around the maypole.

Morris dancers in Derbyshire.

Harvest time

The culmination of all these rituals was the bringing in of the harvest. With the benefits of freezers and imported foods, it is difficult for us to understand the importance of this occasion. The Harvest Festivals celebrated in churches and schools today are a pale imitation of the Harvest Home celebrations of earlier years. These were great occasions with much feasting, drinking and music-making.

"So fill your cups and drink, my boys,
It is our harvest home."

Once again, the novels of Thomas Hardy give us an idea of such country celebrations. *Far From The Madding Crowd* features a Harvest Home feast which went on until the next morning. Like Christmas, Harvest Home was a time when class divisions were relaxed.

Although we are no longer so closely in time with the rhythms of nature, folk music and dance keep alive some memory of these old seasonal celebrations.

PART FOUR

FOLK MUSIC AS A FORM OF REBELLION

During the 1960s, the idea of the "protest song" became very popular. This was linked with the Folk-song Revival, which will be discussed later. In fact, almost all folk music can be classed as a form of protest. It is traditionally the music of those who do not have easy access to political or economic power. It is not the music of military parades or church services. "You can't fill out any kind of a civil service paper and find a green government check in your mailbox for making up and playing folk music and folk-songs" (Woody Guthrie).

Folk music celebrates the triumphs and disasters of ordinary people, and often goes against the values of those in authority.

Life in the countryside was not all thatched cottages and maypole dancing. In 1834, a group of farmworkers in Tolpuddle, Dorset, were sentenced to transportation for attempting to form a trade union. Conditions for agricultural workers were very hard, and they sometimes turned to violence to air their grievances. This picture shows disgruntled workers setting fire to hay-ricks in Kent in 1830.

"The English repertoire offers an astonishingly large number of incitements to drink, a great deal of bawdy and erotic detail, a passion for love-making in the open-air, and a love of dancing, gambling and plain-fun comedy. A strong sense of folk justice runs through, from the wild outlawry of the Robin Hood ballads to the highwaymen, the poachers and the transportation songs of the nineteenth century."
(Sam Richards and Trish Stubbs, *The English Folksinger*, Collins, 1979)

This chapter deals with the attitudes seen in folk music towards the law and towards sex.

Law and order

"The outlaw songs grew in a society divided, poor against rich, villein and small freeholder against landlord, gentry and higher clergy. The heroes on the dodge among the green leaves of the forest represent a kind of dream of the zenith of bow and arrow culture. They are the champions of the down-trodden against the haughty, their weapons pointed towards the dragon of social injustice."
(A.L. Lloyd, *Folk Song in England*, Lawrence & Wishart, 1967)

Robin Hood is, without a doubt, the best-known outlaw in the English tradition. (The ideal of the outlaw who robs the rich in order to help the poor also appears in the Welsh legends of Twm Sion Catti.) No fewer than forty Robin Hood ballads survive in the English folk-song repertoire. Robin Hood provides a link between earlier legends of the "green man" and modern folk heroes. He was possibly based on a genuine outlaw (or even several outlaws), but many of the ballads give him supernatural powers. Others show that, despite being an outlaw, he had a strong sense of what was right and

Dick Turpin's famous ride to York on his horse Black Bess is unlikely ever to have taken place. However, the legend demonstrates the way in which highwaymen were glamorized.

wrong. In "Robin Hood Rescuing Three Squires" a woman asks for Robin's help in rescuing her three sons who are condemned to be hanged. He first asks about their crime:

"What church have they robbed said bold Robin Hood
Or what parish priest have they slain,
What maid have they forced against her own will,
Or with other men's wives have they lain?"

When he finds out that their only crime is to have killed sixteen of the king's deer, Robin agrees to rescue them.

In later years, the tradition of the Robin Hood ballads was transferred to highwaymen. The fact that most of these were ruthless murderers is ignored in folk-song – after all, the people they robbed were rich. Highwaymen are generally portrayed as devoted family men, always anxious to help grey-haired widows and loyal to their comrades. The capture and death of William Brennan, an Irish highwayman hanged in 1804, are celebrated in the following lines:

"A brace of loaded pistols he carried night and day,
He never robbed a poor man upon the King's highway;
But what he'd taken from the rich, like Turpin and Black Bess,
He always did divide it with the widow in distress.

Then Brennan being an outlaw upon the mountains high
The cavalry and infantry to take him they did try.
Brennan lost his forefinger, taken off by a cannon-ball
Then he and his comrades were taken after all.

Farewell unto my wife and to my children
   three
Likewise my aged father, he may shed
   tears for me,
And to my loving mother, who tore her
   hair and cried
Saying, 'I wish that William Brennan in
   the cradle he had died.'"

It is easy to criticize the way that such ballads glamorize the careers of criminals. They have little to do with real people,

On the way to Tyburn. A detail from an engraving by Hogarth (1697-1764). The gallows stood near the site occupied today by the Marble Arch in London.

however. William Brennan, Dick Turpin, Jesse James, Pretty Boy Floyd and Bonnie and Clyde all might have robbed from the rich only because the poor had nothing worth stealing, but as far as folk music is concerned, they were natural heirs to Robin Hood.

The manner of a criminal's death could also be of concern to the folk-singer. Between 1196 and 1783, more than 50,000 people were hung at Tyburn alone, often for offences which would be regarded as fairly trivial today. Poaching, for example, was a capital offence less than two hundred years ago.

"O such a brave fellow there never was yet;
He must suffer to be hanged before he would split.
He would suffer to be hanged, the keepers well know,
And he fought in the covert some winters ago."
(From a folk-song about poaching collected by Ralph Vaughan Williams in Essex)

Poachers faced severe penalties if they were caught.

Executions were great public occasions and condemned criminals were expected to put on a performance for the crowd. A criminal about to be hanged could create a longlasting impression on the popular imagination with a good show on the way to the gallows or an impressive last speech. Such gallows farewells are a common theme in folk music, and some have even travelled across the Atlantic.

"But when I'm dead and carried to my grave,
A pleasant funeral let me have,
Six highwaymen to carry me:
Give them broadswords and sweet liberty.

Six blooming girls to bear up my pall,
Give them white gloves and pink ribbons all.
When I'm dead they may tell the truth;
There goes a wild and wicked youth."

Those lines were collected by Ralph Vaughan Williams in Suffolk, but very similar sentiments are expressed in the Irish ballad "The Unfortunate Rake" and the American songs "Streets Of Laredo" and "Saint James's Infirmary".

"When I die I want six crap shooters to be my pallbearers
Three pretty women to sing a song;
Put a jazzband on rny hearse wagon,
And raise hell as we ride along."

("St James's Infirmary", sometimes also known as "Gambler's Blues")

Not all criminals were hanged, of course. Two hundred years ago, the British government had the idea of transporting

Those sentenced to transportation faced appalling conditions on the voyage to Australia. They were kept in cages below deck and many died before they reached land.

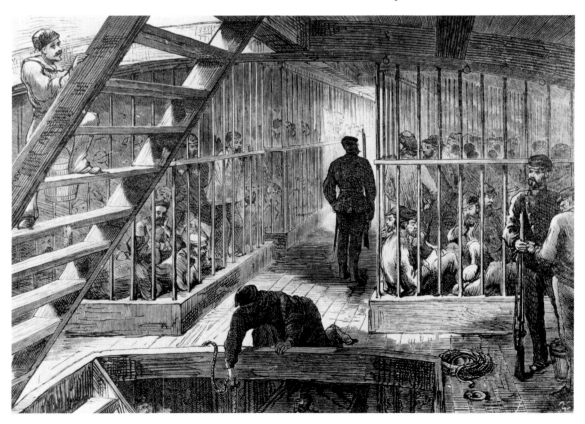

convicted men and women to Australia. Many folk-songs tell of the hardships of the long voyage and the cruel conditions at the end of it. Perhaps the best-known is "Van Dieman's Land":

"It was at the March Assizes to the bar
    we did repair.
Like Job we stood with patience to hear
    our sentence there;
There being some old offenders, which
    made our case go hard,
My sentence was for fourteen years,
    then I was sent on board.

The fifteenth of September, 'twas then
    we made the land
At four o'clock we went on shore all
    chained hand in hand;
To see our fellow sufferers we felt I can't
    tell how,
Some chained unto a harrow and others
    to a plough.

No shoes or stockings they had on, nor
    hat they had to wear
Leather breeches and linen drawers,
    their feet and hands were bare,
They chained them up by two and two
    like horses in a team,
Their driver he stood over them with his
    malacca cane."

Sex

There is little room in folk music for songs about happy relationships. Love songs are generally sad, telling of dead or jilted lovers or ones left holding the baby. The cruel father who parts the young lovers is a common figure. In "The Old Miser", for example, the wicked father sells his daughter's lover to a sea captain. The young man is kidnapped, taken on board ship and never sees his sweetheart again. The press-gang appears frequently in folk-songs, with women lamenting the fate of their loved ones forced to join the navy.

---

press-gang: *a detachment of men used to force civilians into service in the navy or army.*

"It chanced her aged parents they
    came for to know
That the ploughboy did court their
    daughter Jane
A press-gang they did send and
    pressed the ploughboy away
For to send him to the wars to be slain,
    to be slain,
For to send him to the wars to be slain."

In this song, "The Pretty Ploughboy", widely known in country districts during the nineteenth century, the victim of the press-gang is rescued by his lover.

Other songs tell of lovers who have gone away to fight in foreign wars:

"It was down in the meadows where
    violets are blue
I saw pretty Polly a-milking her cow
And the song that she sang made all the
    grove to ring.
O Billy's gone from me to serve George
    the king.
And I wish that the wars were all over,
Crying O that the wars were all over."
("I Wish That The Wars Were All Over",
collected by Sabine Baring-Gould in
1893)

This song dates from the years of the American War of Independence.

There are many bawdy folk-songs extolling the pleasures of sex, though these were largely ignored by the Victorian folk-song collectors.

"I am a young dairy-maid buxom and
    bright,
In minding my dairy I take great delight
In making of butter and cheese that is
    new
And a young man to play with my how
    d'you do."
("The Buxom Dairy Maid")

The use of double meanings was common, as in this song collected by J.G. Guyer in Hampshire:

"Come all you rakish bachelors, come listen to my tale.
I've got a cottage neat and snug I'm putting up for sale.
It's in a pleasant valley with a rising hill above
And a crystal stream of water is a-running through a grove.
Then occupy my cottage for it is in good repair.
It has a pleasant entrance and will suit you to a hair."

This liberal attitude towards sex did not extend to pregnancy, which was almost invariably regarded as the woman's fault.

"Is that the promise I made to you
Which I never intend to do?
For I never intend to marry a girl
Whose heart's too easy to woo . . . .

Well if you are in child by me,
Which I may suppose you be,
Just wrap it up in its petticoats warm
And doddle it on your knee . . . .

Then if that you must stay at home
Singing hushy bye baby-i-o,
You just think back how it all came about
And you blame your own free will."
("As I Was Out A-Walking")

"So come pretty maidens where ever you be
With courting young fellows don't make yourselves free,
For if you should do so you'll rue the sad day
When you met with the like of young Ramble-Away"
("Young Ramble-Away")

"Bonny Robin", collected in Norfolk by Ralph Vaughan Williams, shows that the same attitude was not directed at young men:

"I hastened my horses to walk by her side,

The roads being dirty I asked her to ride,
I heaved her up gently, lay her at her ease,
Then it's 'Come and lie with me young man, if you please.'

But if this young damsel should ask me my name,
There's some call me Robin and some call me Ben,
But as for the other one I dare not tell
For fear this young damsel should chance for to swell."

There are songs, however, in which the woman comes out best. This is particularly the case when the would-be seducer is of a higher social class. A widespread example is a song known variously as "Lovely Joan", "The Farmer In Leicester" or "The Crafty Farmer". The common theme of all of these is the outwitting of a rich young man (a highwayman in some versions) by a farmer's daughter. She not only escapes his clutches but steals his money as well. In "The Dew Is On The Grass", a song from Suffolk, a young gentleman, sure of his charms, is mocked by the woman he attempts to seduce:

"There is a cock in my father's yard,
He will not tread the hen sir,
And I do think in my very heart
That you are one of them, sir."

It is in songs about marriage that women really come into their own. In such songs, men are generally regarded as idle, drunken and stupid. "Hecketty Pecketty", collected by Cecil Sharp in 1904, is a warning against marriage.

"Hecketty pecketty needles and pins,
matrimony and sorrow begins
A maid I am and a maid I'll be, Man's love to me is all my eye.
Think I'll bide home to wash and brew,
to mend his holes in his stockings too
While he is out to the public house and heaven be praised I've found him out"

KITTY TYRRELL,

SUNG BY   **IRISH BALLAD,**   Mʳ G. GENGE

WRITTEN BY   COMPOSED BY

CHAˢ JEFFERYS   **C. W. GLOVER.**

ENT. STA. HALL   Pⁱ 2/.

LONDON, C. JEFFERYS 21, SOHO SQUARE.

Nineteenth-century romantic songs took a rather sentimental view of love. Folk music was generally more down-to-earth.

"I'll Be No Submissive Wife" is a strongly worded declaration of women's rights:

> "I'll be no submissive wife, no not I, no not I.
> I'll not be a slave for life, no not I.
> Think you on a wedding day, that I'd say as other say,
> Love, honour and obey? No not I, no not I.
> Love, honour and obey? No, not I."

Drunken husbands get little sympathy:

> "Then he came home in a terrible rage
> But she was ready the foe to engage.
> She plucked up her spirits and he did begin
> She knocked him down with a rolling pin.
>
> He hollered aloud, she tore his clothes,
> She blacked his eye and broked off his nose,
> You villain, she cried, no more of your airs
> And slap she bundled him over the stairs."

("The Drunken Man", collected by Cecil Sharp, 1908)

Not surprisingly, the man in this particular song promises to mend his ways and never get drunk again. Songs about patient wives waiting at home for the return of their wandering husbands are rare. On the other hand, songs in which wives become fed up with their husbands and take a lover are very common. Sympathy is almost always with the wife, and the husband is often made to look foolish.

In "Timothy Briggs The Barber", Timothy Briggs, having got married, has second thoughts within a fortnight. He goes to see the "wooden-legged parson named Jonathan Sly" who conducted the marriage service, and asks for his help:

> "And since you have made us two into one
> I've come for to see if we can't be undone."

The parson promises to see what he can do and the next day, when Briggs arrives home, he finds "the parson with Betty on top of his knee". He angrily asks Sly what is going on, to which the parson replies:

> "Oh you said that you wanted undoing, my man
> Don't you see I'm a-trying as fast as I can."

The parson who is not as good as he ought to be is a common character in folk-songs, a tradition which can be traced back to the Middle Ages. In Chaucer's *Canterbury Tales*, the Pardoner claims to have a potion which will cure jealousy. It is so effective that a man would believe his wife innocent of adultery, even if he had knowledge of her having had affairs with two or three priests!

Another tradition which goes back a long way is the "May and December" story, in which an old man marries a young woman who is unfaithful to him. (Once again, examples of this can be found in *The Canterbury Tales*.) This is a common theme in folk-songs:

> "When he got into bed,
> All the days of my life,
> When he got into bed,
> Hey diddle dee,
> When he got into bed
> He lay like a lump of lead,
> Girls for my sake never wed an old man.

Chaucer: *Geoffrey Chaucer (1340-1400). An English poet, best known for his work* The Canterbury Tales.

When he was fast asleep
Out of bed I did creep
Into the arms of a nice young man.

Then we did sport and play
Until the break of day
Then I went back to the silly old man."
("Never Marry An Old Man", collected
by Cecil Sharp, 1904)

These nocturnal meetings were not always
safe, of course. The song "Go From My
Window" has been in circulation since at
least the sixteenth century. In it, a young
woman warns her lover to stay away
because her husband is at home:

"Begone, begone, my Willy, my Billy,
Begone my love and my dear.
Oh the wind is in the west
And the cuckoo's in his nest,
And you cannot have a lodging here."

There is also a Welsh song, "*Rhybudd i'r
Carwr*" ("A Warning To The Lover"), which
has very similar words:

"Y llong a aeth o'r porthladd
Heb gapten ar y bwrdd,
Am hyn mae'n edifar gen i;
Y gwynt o'r gorwel chwyth,
A'r frân sydd ar y nyth."
(The ship has left the port without the
captain on board, the wind blows from
the horizon, the crow is on its nest, and
so there's no room for you.)

Unfaithful wives did not always escape,
and in "The Old Woman In Yorkshire" it is
the husband who does the outwitting. The
old woman in question loves her husband
dearly but "another man twice as well".
She obtains a potion which makes her
husband blind and this makes him so
miserable that he says he wants to drown
himself. She offers to lead him down to the
river and push him in. As she steps forward
to shove him, he stands aside and she
tumbles into the river.

"Good Lord, O she did holler, good
Lord, O she did bawl.
The old man said: I am so blind I can't
see nowt at all.
She swam until she floated unto the
river's brim.
The old man took his walking stick and
shoved her further in."

The rough justice meted out in this song is
a common theme in folk music. This folk
justice is based not necessarily on any
written law, but rather on a strong sense of
what can be seen to be fair. Outlaw songs
and bawdy songs illustrate an attitude to
life which never totally accepts the
authority of those who have put themselves in charge.

PART FIVE

INDUSTRIAL FOLK-SONGS

The Victorian folk-song collectors felt that they were preserving an art form which was facing extinction. So far as they were concerned, folk-song was the music of the countryside. The growth of towns and the decline in the number of people employed in agriculture therefore meant the end of folk music. In fact, from the earliest days of the Industrial Revolution, workers in the towns were creating their own folk-songs; songs which reflected new conditions and ways of life but which retained many of the traditional features and concerns of folk music.

There have always been folk-songs about work, of course, ranging from ploughmen's songs to sea shanties, but it is in the industrial songs that a real group identity is expressed. Many of these songs are not about an industry as a whole but about one sub-section of workers within that industry. They display a great pride in the skills of the group and are full of

Women working on power looms in 1844. The picture gives no idea of the incredible noise these machines must have made, nor of the dangerous working conditions.

technical details which often mean little to an outsider. The finest examples of industrial folk-song are those which stem from the cotton and coalmining industries.

"The Bury New Loom", a song from the end of the eighteenth century, contains many references to the technical processes involved in weaving and, in common with many early industrial folk-songs, gives them a sexual double meaning.

"As I walked between Bolton and Bury, 'twas on a moonshiny night
I met with a buxom young weaver whose company gave me delight
She says, "Young fellow, come tell me if your level and rule are in tune
Come, give me an answer correct, can you get up and square my new loom?"

The late eighteenth and early nineteenth centuries were a boom time for the cotton industry. The growth of the British Empire provided a cheap source of raw materials and a massive new market for the finished cloth. Inventions such as James Hargreaves' "spinning-jenny" and Richard Arkwright's "water frame" opened the way for mass-production. The new cotton mills in the north of England attracted workers from surrounding rural areas, rapidly swelling the size of the towns. The population of Bolton, for example, doubled between 1773 and 1786.

In 1790, Arkwright developed a loom powered by steam:

"Where are the girls? I'll tell you plain,
The girls have gone to weave by steam,
And if you find 'em, you must rise at dawn,
And trudge to the factory in the early morn."

A contemporary cartoon of a Luddite leader disguised as a woman. Notice the factory blazing in the background.

The invention of large new machines did away with the need for many of the old skills and this caused great resentment. As early as 1779, rioters destroyed one of Arkwright's cotton mills. In 1811, a serious outbreak of rioting occurred in Nottingham and West Yorkshire. The rioters were known as Luddites, after one of their leaders, Ned Ludd. Several mills were destroyed, many people were killed and large numbers of rioters were tried and executed.

The hardships suffered by cotton workers and their fight for better conditions were the themes of many industrial folk-songs from 1820 onwards, as the initial boom years came to an end. One of the best-known of these songs is "The Four Loom Weaver":

"I'm a poor cotton weaver as many one knows
I've nowt t'eat i'the house and I've wore out my cloes."

The coal-mining industry has produced a wealth of songs about industrial struggles. Some were fund-raising efforts, written to put the miners' case across to the public, as in this example from 1892:

"In our Durham county I am sorry for to say
That hunger and starvation is increasing every day
For want of food and coals, we know not what to do
But with your kind assistance we will stand the battle through."

Other coal-mining songs were calls for solidarity and warnings to those who attempted to break ranks during a strike and go back to work.

"Now Dicky, was thou at the meeting today?
Aw look'd, but aw saw nought o' thou by the way

A mass meeting of striking textile workers in Blackburn, 1861.

Aw hope that thou's not turnin' cowardly noo,
Or thinkin' a gannin' doon coal-pit to hew."
(from the Durham strike of 1831)

"The Dirty Blackleg Miner" is a song widely known throughout the British coal-fields and it has also travelled across to the United States.

---

blackleg: *a person who continues to work when a strike is taking place. Also known as a scab.*

"So join the union while ye may
Don't wait until your dying day
For that may not be far away
Ye dirty blackleg miners."

Industrial folk-songs often attempted to tell the public the truth about particular industries, especially when official reports did not seem to be frank enough. There are a number of songs about mining disasters, while others tell of hazards and difficult working conditions encountered.

"All the day long you may say we are buried
Deprived of the light and the warmth of the sun
And often at night from our bed we are hurried
The water is in, and barefoot we run."
("The Collier Lass")

Striking miners argue their case. An artist's impression of the Preston strike of the 1850s.

"To be a Sheffield grinder it is no easy
   trade
There's more than you'd imagine in the
   grinding of a blade
The strongest man among us is old at
   thirty-two
For there's few that brave the hardships
   that we poor grinders do."
("The Sheffield Grinder's Song")

The first of these songs dates from the time when children were employed in coal-mines. The second is about conditions in the Sheffield cutlery industry during the nineteenth century. As the song goes on to point out, the grinders were "breathing dust and steel" every working day, while pieces of broken grindstone often caused serious injuries. Industrial hazards were not confined to the nineteenth century, however, as shown by the following two songs, both written in the 1960s.

"Been working at dye-works for nearly
   five years
Been changing the naphthas that give
   yer the pap
They send it from Ikey for us to shove in
This vitriol and chloric as makes us all
   thin."
("The Clayton Analine Song" by Pete
Smith)

"Pap" is papilloma of the bladder, a cancer caused by working with certain chemicals. "Ikey" means ICI. The use of "naphtha" (beta-naphthyl-amine) was banned in 1967.

Queueing for coal during the 1873 South Wales miners' strike. This scene is in Merthyr Tydfil, one of many small villages which grew into major industrial towns during the nineteenth century.

"There's overtime and bonus
   opportunities galore
Young lads like the money and they all
   come back for more
But soon you're knocking on and look
   older than you should
For every bob made in this job you pay
   with flesh and blood."
("Chemical Workers' Song" by Ron Angel)

Not all industrial folk-songs deal with strikes or hardships. There are many which express pride in the workers' skills. The mining industry in particular has produced a number of songs about the exploits of superhuman workmen. Some of these have taken on mythical qualities as if their spirits still haunted the mines. Thus, when there were unexplained noises in a South Wales pit, the miners would attribute it to "Big Isaac" working somewhere still. The closure of many mines since the 1960s has produced songs which pay affectionate tribute to a former workplace. Albert Pit at Abram in Lancashire was closed in 1965:

"Owd Albert's gone, his days are done.
His gates are shuttered fast, he lies in
   peace.
Through summer's warm and winter's
   storm
There's no-one to disturb his blackened
   sleep."

The Welsh singer, Max Boyce, wrote a song which summed up neatly the mixed feelings aroused by the closure of a pit. As he says himself, "the song has always meant a great deal to me, because my father was killed in a colliery explosion and I worked for many years underground myself".

"They came down here from London
   because our output's low
Briefcases full of bank clerks that have
   never been below.
And they'll close the valley's oldest
   mine, pretending that they're sad
But don't you worry, Butty Bach, we're
   really very glad.

My clean-clothes'-locker's empty now,
  I've thrown away the key
And I've sold my boots and muffler and
  my lamp-check one-five-three
But I can't forget the times we had, the
  laughing midst the fear
'Cos every time I cough I get a mining
  souvenir . . . .

'Cos it's hard, Duw it's hard.
It's harder than they will ever know.
And if ham was underground, would it
  be twelve bob a pound?
The pithead baths is a supermarket
  now."

(from *I Was There*, Weidenfeld and
Nicolson, 1979)

PART SIX

OLD SONGS IN A NEW LAND

The folk music of the United States of America is an incredibly rich mixture of different cultures and traditions. It includes the music of the original inhabitants of the country – the so-called "Red Indians" – as well as that of later European and African arrivals. The European immigrants came from Britain, Ireland, Spain, France, Italy, Germany, Scandinavia, Eastern Europe and Russia. Some of these different cultures borrowed from each other while others remained isolated. It would be impossible to examine all of these forms of music here, but it is important to remember that they exist. This chapter is concerned mainly with American folk music which stems from the British and Irish traditions.

The first British and Irish settlers in North America carried with them folk-songs in their current form. Gradually, however, these were adapted to fit the new conditions. The Declaration of Independence in 1776, for example, provided the inspiration for a host of

An artist's impression of the Pilgrim Fathers landing in America in 1620. Their landing site was Cape Cod in what is now Massachusetts.

The Appalachian Mountains stretch 2,560 km from Maine to Alabama.

songs, many of them based on traditional British and Irish ballads, extolling the virtues of the United States of America and the vices of "Old England". Throughout the nineteenth century this process of Americanization continued. The most important aspect was the development of "hillbilly" music in the Appalachian Mountains – an area which covers parts of the states of Kentucky, Virginia, Carolina and Tennessee. The basic instruments of this music are the mandolin, the banjo, the violin and, occasionally, the accordion, but the most important are the dulcimer and the autoharp. The singing style is very nasal and generally high-pitched, with the occasional use of yodels. The themes of hillbilly songs are very similar to those of English ballads, with the inclusion in the plot of as much detail as possible. The American songs tend to be more gory, though. Many are concerned with violence – rape, murder and hangings are common. Often murder is committed by a jilted lover who is then hung, as in "Tom Dooley" and "The Banks Of The Ohio" ("I killed the only one I love, because she would not marry me"). Many songs, such

---

dulcimer: *a stringed instrument of the zither family, played with small hammers.*

---

autoharp: *a member of the zither family equipped with button-controlled dampers which can prevent certain strings from sounding, thus allowing chords to be played. It is plucked with the fingers or with a plectrum.*

as "Tom Dooley", are based on actual events. "Polly Williams" describes an occurrence of 1810, when a man from a wealthy family seduced a country girl, lured her to a place called White Rocks and threw her to her death.

"Come all ye good people who saw this
    object,
Don't add nor diminish, deceive nor
    correct,
This honored young lady was found in a
    gore
And her flesh by this traitor all mangled
    and tore."

Between 1916 and 1918, Cecil Sharp visited the United States and in 1919 published his English Folk Songs from the Southern Appalachians, *identifying the region as a vast storehouse of traditional music. This photograph was taken in Virginia in the 1920s.*

The mood of the songs is rarely mournful, however, and often quite light-hearted. A more refined version of hillbilly music was developed in Kentucky. Known as "blue-grass", it is notable for the role it gives to the banjo players, who developed a high degree of virtuosity.

Another form of American folk music which developed during the nineteenth century was the cowboy song. It is sometimes difficult to disentangle the reality of the cowboys' lives from the mythical portrait of them shown in countless films. In reality cowboys received miserable wages in return for hard and dangerous work. It was a lonely life, and cowboy songs reflect this.

"I ain't got no father
To buy the clothes I wear
I'm a poor lonesome cowboy
And a long way from home.

I ain't got no mother
To mend the clothes I wear
I'm a poor lonesome cowboy
And a long way from home."

Other songs deal with the extremes of weather which the cowboys had to endure.

"Oh, the devil in hell they say he was
   chained,
And there for a thousand years he
   remained
He neither complained nor did he groan
But decided he'd start up a hell of his
   own,
Where he could torment the souls of
   men
Without being shut in a prison pen;
So he asked the Lord if he had any sand
Left over from making this great land.

The colourful myths of cowboy life bear little relation to the harsh reality.

The Lord He said, 'Yes, I have plenty on
   hand
But it's away down south on the Rio
   Grande
And, to tell you the truth, the stuff is so
   poor,
I doubt if 'twill do for hell any more,'
The Devil went down and looked over
   the truck
And he said if it came as a gift he was
   stuck
For when he'd examined it carefully and
   well
He decided the place was too dry for a
   hell."
("Hell In Texas")

45

There are also a number of songs about larger-than-life characters, beautiful women and the joys of finally riding into a town after weeks out on the prairie.

"Whee-oop! Whoop-eee!
Does anyone find any flies on me?
Say! I'm the king of the cow-puncher
  clan,
A sizeable sort of a fightin' man,
With my lungs full of air, an' my pockets
  full of cash,
Achin' an' longin' to make it flash,
Ready for anythin', wise or rash;
Come on, you fellers, the round's on
  me!"
("In Town")

Country and western music emerged in the 1920s as a mixture of hillbilly music and the remnants of cowboy music. The earliest country and western stars, among them JIMMIE RODGERS and HANK WILLIAMS SENIOR, remained close to the folk roots of the music. Increasingly, however, the influence of record companies, television and all the other trappings of show business became evident. Whatever its merits, country and western can no longer be regarded as a form of folk music.

Throughout the nineteenth century, the United States expanded westwards. The songs of those who travelled west reflect their day-to-day concerns. Many of them are concerned with the ways in which travelling was made easier. For example, settlers travelling into Tennessee and Ohio had to pass through the Cumberland Gap, a break in the high wall of the Appalachian Mountains. In 1795, the state government approved a project to construct a road through the Gap, an event celebrated in song.

Daniel Boone escorting pioneers over the Cumberland Gap. A painting by George Caleb Bingham (1811-79)

"Lay down boys, and take a little nap,
Fourteen miles to the Cumberland Gap.
Cumberland Gap, Cumberland Gap,
Fourteen miles to the Cumberland Gap.

The first white man in Cumberland Gap,
Was Doctor Walker, an English chap.

Cumberland Gap with its cliff and rocks
Home of the panther, bear and fox"

[and so on, for at least eighteen verses
. . . .]

The construction of the Erie Canal, opened in 1825, made it possible to travel by water from New York to the Great Lakes, passing through the Mohawk Gap in the Appalachian Mountains. This feat of engineering is celebrated in a number of songs. John and Alan Lomax devote a whole section to Erie Canal songs in their collection *American Ballads and Folk Songs* (MacMillan, New York, 1934).

"We were forty miles from Albany
Forget it I never shall,
What a terrible storm we had one night
On the Erie Canal.

Oh, the Erie was a-rising
The gin was getting low,
And I scarcely think
We'll get a drink
Till we get to Buffalo."
("The Erie")

"You may talk about pleasures
And trips on the lake,
But a trip on the Erie,
You bet takes the cake,
With the beefsteak as tough
As a fighting dog's neck
And the flies playing tag
With the cook on the deck."
("A Trip On The Erie")

The Erie Canal, about 1835.

48

In the second half of the nineteenth century, westwards migration was given a further boost by the discovery of gold in California. Thousands set out to seek their fortunes, lured by the promise of easy money.

"Then ho boys ho, to Californy-o
There's plenty of gold, so I've been told
On the banks of the Sacramento."

A later variant of these lines shows the reality of the gold-rush:

"Then ho boys ho, to Californy-o,
There's plenty of stones and dead
    men's bones
On the banks of the Sacramento."

The most important improvement in transport and communications, of course, was the coming of the railroad. Train songs of one form or another form an enormous part of American folk music. There are songs about the building of the railroad, the most famous of these being "John Henry". This superhuman tunnel-borer died, according to legend, after attempting to beat the speed of a steam drill with his hand drill. Variations on the ballad of John Henry appear in both white and black folk music. There are also songs about the railroad disasters, for example, "Casey Jones".

Panning for gold in California

The greatest number of train songs, however, are about hoboes. The hobo is the hero of American folk music, travelling constantly by hitching free rides on freight trains. Hoboes knew by heart the time-tables of all the main routes and the time it took to get to various destinations.

"Standing on the platform,
Smoking a cheap cigar,
A-listening for the next freight train
To catch an empty car,

My pocketbook was empty,
My heart was full of pain,
Ten thousand miles away from home,
A-bumming the railroad train."

Union Pacific train in Western Kansas in about 1870.

The most famous of all the hobo songs, "Hallelujah, I'm a Bum", was found scribbled on the wall of a Kansas City jail.

"Oh, why don't I work like other men do?
How the hell can I work when the skies
    are so blue?
Hallelujah, I'm a bum,
Hallelujah, bum again,
Hallelujah, give's a handout,
Revive us again . . . .

Oh, the winter is over and we're all out of
    jail,
We're tired of walking and hungry as
    hell.

Oh, I ride box cars and I ride fast mails,
When it's cold in the winter I sleep in the
    jails.

50

The industrialization of the United States in the late nineteenth century created vast wealth, which went into the pockets of a relatively small number of people. Working people saw little of the benefits. They were forced to live in slums and to work in dangerous conditions, and were likely to be laid off at a moment's notice. In addition to this, vast numbers of immigrants, who would work for even lower wages, were flooding into the United States from the poorest parts of Europe. American workers organized themselves into unions for their own protection, braving the open hostility of employers and the government. During the last twenty years of the nineteenth century there were over 30,000 strikes, many of them involving considerable violence.

The American Federation of Labor, founded in the 1880s, mainly represented skilled workers and sought to co-operate with employers rather than fight them. On the other hand, the Industrial Workers of the World, founded in 1905 and popularly known as the "Wobblies", attempted to organize all workers. The Wobblies used folk-songs to get their message across, issuing them in the form of a book called *Songs to Fan the Flames of Discontent*. Many of these songs were written by JOE HILL, one of the most famous figures in American union history. Born Joel Emmanuel Hagglund in Sweden, he emigrated to the United States in 1901. In 1910, having changed his name to Joseph Hillstrom, he became an active member of the Industrial Workers of the World, putting his songwriting talents at the organization's disposal. "Casey Jones, the Union Scab" tells of the strike-breaker who goes to heaven when he dies. The Angels' union, however, refuses to let him in and he is sent to spy in hell. "The White Slave" is about a young girl forced into prostitution:

> "Who is to blame? You know his name
> It's the boss who pays starvation
> wages."

Joe Hill was eventually found guilty of murder and executed in 1915. The circumstances of the trial were suspect, to say the least, and even the American President, Woodrow Wilson, appealed for a pardon.

The most active singer in the union movement in the 1930s and 1940s, and arguably the greatest folk-singer America has produced, was WOODY GUTHRIE. Guthrie was born in 1912 in the small town of Okemah, Oklahoma. He spent much of his life on the road, taking odd jobs where he could find them and also earning money from playing his guitar and singing. His early life was full of tragedies – his sister was killed in a fire, his mother died in hospital after a nervous breakdown, and his father was badly injured in yet another

Migrant workers in New Jersey. The wealth created by the industrialization of the United States was not evenly distributed.

fire. Oklahoma suffered more than any other state in the Depression of the 1930s. In addition to the financial difficulties, farmers suffered several years of very dry weather. Severe dust-storms swept away the topsoil, making the land useless for agriculture. Thousands of people migrated to California seeking work as fruit-pickers. When they arrived at the California state line, however, the "Okies", as they were known, were often turned back by the police. They were forced to live in shanty towns and suffered extreme hardships. Guthrie documented this period in a series of songs, collectively known as the *Dust Bowl Ballads*. These include "Talking Dust Bowl Blues", "I'm Blowin' Down This Old Dusty Road", "Dust

At the end of Route 66, families from Oklahoma found themselves forced to live in makeshift camps like the one pictured here.

Cain't Kill Me", "I Am A Dust Bowl Refugee", "Dust Pneumonia Blues" and "I Ain't Got No Home In This World Anymore". "The Great Dust-Storm" describes such a storm first-hand, relating how the dust blows through the smallest cracks, burying fences and farm machinery.

In 1937, Guthrie received a request from the Federal authorities to write a series of songs about the construction of two huge dams on the Columbia River. The authorities wanted songs which glorified the construction project, but what they got were songs glorifying the people who were actually working on the dams. Guthrie became increasingly involved with union activities, making many appearances at strike meetings and demonstrations. He also worked with other singers, among them CISCO HOUSTON, PETE SEEGER and the black singers LEADBELLY and SONNY TERRY. His songs often combined black and white traditions, containing strong elements of blues and gospel, cowboy songs and hillbilly music.

> "I mix up old tunes; I wheel them and I deal them; and I shuffle them out across my barking board; I use half of two tunes, one third of three tunes, one tenth of ten tunes. I always save back my notes and words left over and pound them out to poke fun at the Democrats and the Republicans and those Wall Street ramblers."
> (Woody Guthrie, *Born To Win*, MacMillan, New York)

In 1954 Guthrie was admitted to hospital suffering from Huntington's chorea, a disease which attacks the nervous system and which causes progressive paralysis.

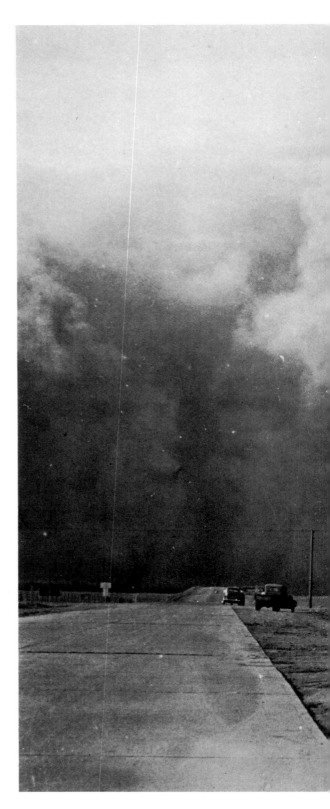

A dust-storm approaching the town of Springfield in Oklahoma on 21 May 1937. According to eyewitness accounts, the town was plunged into total darkness for over half an hour.

He died in 1967, after twelve years of constant pain. Apart from the importance of his own songs, Guthrie was a great influence on a new generation of American singers. When asked if he thought that folk music was on its way out, he had the following to say:

"As long as we've got wrecks, disasters, cyclones, hurricanes, explosions, lynchings, trade union troubles, high prices and low pay, as long as we've got cops in uniform battling with union pickets on strike, folk-songs and folk ballads are on their way in."

PART SEVEN

FOLK MUSIC TODAY

During the early 1950s, American folk music, black and white, was far more widely known in Britain than traditional British music. Skiffle – a form of music based on the American jug bands of the 1930s – was very popular. Skiffle groups used very simple instruments – a bass made from a tea chest and a broom handle, for example – and their repertoire was largely American. The songs "Tom Dooley" and "The Cumberland Gap", mentioned earlier, were great favourites, as was the music of Leadbelly and Woody Guthrie. Then, EWAN MACCOLL was approached by the BBC to make a series of eight radio documentaries using folksong. The programmes proved popular and MacColl started putting on concerts as well. He ran a folk club in London where he insisted that singers should perform songs from their own tradition. Gradually these different strands came together and the folk revival was born.

At first, folk clubs concerned themselves with saving and passing on traditional music. There was a conscious effort to make recordings of older singers while there was still time. HARRY COX, a Norfolk farm labourer, and SAM LARNER, who made his first recordings at the age of 79, are perhaps the most widely known. THE COPPER FAMILY, from Rottingdean in Sussex, sing in harmony, using arrangements that have existed in their family for over a hundred years. There were also younger musicians who learnt traditional

---

jug band: *a band using simple home-made instruments. The bass line was provided by a player blowing across the neck of a stone whisky jug.*

---

songs in order to keep them alive. MARTIN CARTHY was introduced to folk music by the skiffle craze. He had a great impact on the folk revival and was also involved in the electric folk music of the 1960s.

In the 1960s, there were attempts to "dress up" the music in various ways. The use of electric instruments in folk music began in the United States. In 1965, BOB DYLAN outraged many of his fans when he appeared at the Newport Folk Festival with a rock band backing him. It was with this electric music, however, that he achieved his greatest success. For a year or two, "folk rock" was very popular, though in reality, little of the music had much to do with folk. In Britain, there was a more serious attempt to perform traditional music in a more modern setting. FAIRPORT CONVENTION was formed in 1967 and their *Liege and Lief* album, released in 1969, was a great commercial success. STEELEYE SPAN stayed closer to the folk tradition and did not add a drummer to their line-up for several years. PENTANGLE was folk music's answer to the rock "super-groups" of the period, and included such well-respected musicians as BERT JANSCH and JOHN RENBOURN. The problem faced by all these groups was that, as they became more popular, the line between electric folk and rock music became increasingly blurred. They did, on the other hand, introduce traditional music to an audience who might never have heard it otherwise.

At the other extreme, there were musicians who attempted to revive interest in medieval instruments. In 1969 SHIRLEY COLLINS released an album entitled *Anthems in Eden* in which she was accompanied by musicians playing rebecs, crumhorns, sackbuts, viols and recorders. Following the success of this album, a number of "medieval" groups emerged, among them GRYPHON, CITY WAITES and AMAZING BLONDEL (who were more famous for the dirty jokes they told between songs than for their actual music). Shirley Collins, meanwhile, went on to combine English folk music with such elements as jazz, blues and Indian music.

Both electric and medieval folk music had run out of steam by the early 1970s, but by then a new controversy was raging in folk clubs – over the performance of "contemporary" folk-songs. The argument was about whether folk-singers should merely be preserving what had gone before or whether they should be writing new material. There seems to be no satisfactory answer to this question – it depends largely upon what definition of folk music is adopted. Some composed songs, such as those of Ewan MacColl and Ralph McTell, have been accepted into the folk repertoire, while others have been rejected. Traditional singers, of course, did not have this problem. They sang the songs which their audience wanted to hear and did not worry about notions of authenticity. If we define folk music as music created by a community for that community, then there is a strong case for saying that the true late twentieth-century folk-songs are to be found not in folk clubs, but on picket lines and football terraces.

An important recent development has been the growth in interest in the folk music of other countries. This has not been confined to folk clubs, but has been prompted by musicians in other spheres looking for new ideas. Modern recording techniques make music from all over the world freely available to us. In the 1950s, those who were bored with commercially produced music turned to the British and Irish folk traditions. Their modern counterparts can turn to the traditions of many different cultures. When the Israeli singer OFRA HAZA can have a Top Ten hit with an arrangement of a seventeenth-century Yemenite folk-song, perhaps we are on the way to the creation of a world folk music.

---

rebec: *a bowed string instrument.*

---

crumhorn: *a double-reed instrument.*

---

sackbut: *an early form of trombone.*

---

viol: *a bowed string instrument.*

Yemenite: *Yemen is the south-west part of the Arabian peninsula. The Yemenite Jewish community is one of the oldest in the world. The majority of Yemenite Jews now live in Israel.*

MAPS

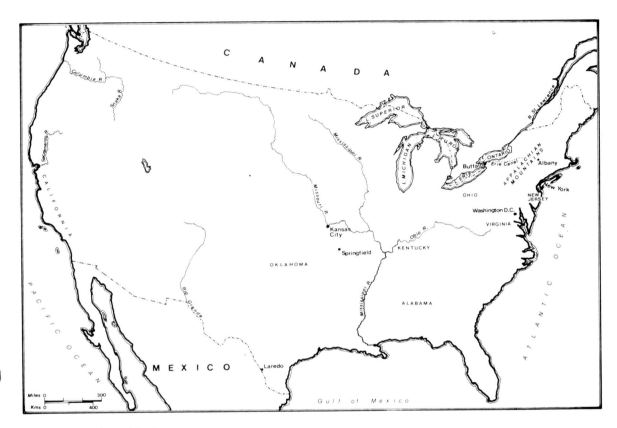

Places mentioned in the text.

Places mentioned in the text.

DATE LIST

1066 — Norman conquest of England
1169 — Normans begin conquest of Ireland
1284 — Norman conquest of Wales completed
1314 — Battle of Bannockburn: Robert Bruce gains Scottish independence
1362 — English becomes the official language in England
1381 — Peasants' Revolt in England
1485 — Beginning of Tudor period in England
1492 — Christopher Columbus reaches West Indies
1513 — Battle of Flodden: James IV of Scotland defeated by English
1603 — Union of England and Scotland
1620 — Pilgrim Fathers settle in New England
1642 — English Civil War
1649 — Oliver Cromwell puts down rebellions in Ireland
1692 — Massacre of Glencoe: English revenge for Highland uprising
1733 — John Kay invents flying shuttle, first of the great textile inventions
1746 — Battle of Culloden: Jacobites defeated
1769 — Richard Arkwright erects spinning mill
1776 — American Declaration of Independence
1783 — American Independence recognized
1789 — French Revolution
1800 — Union of Britain and Ireland
1811 — Luddite riots
1825 — Stockton to Darlington Railway opened
1834 — Tolpuddle Martyrs transported

1840 — Last convicts land in Australia
1846 — Famine in Ireland
1848 — USA makes territorial gains from Mexico
     — Gold discovered in California
1861 — American Civil War
1865 — Slavery abolished in USA
1871 — Trades Unions legalized in Britain
1876 — Battle of Little Big Horn: last major victory by American Indians
1906 — San Francisco destroyed by earthquake and fire
1914 — Outbreak of First World War
1916 — Easter Uprising in Ireland
1917 — Russian Revolution
1918 — End of First World War
1921 — Irish Free State established
1926 — General Strike in Britain
1929 — Wall Street Crash
1939 — Outbreak of Second World War
1941 — Japanese attack on Pearl Harbor. USA enters war
1945 — End of Second World War
1950 — Korean War
1965 — First US bombing raids on North Vietnam
1969 — British soldiers sent to Northern Ireland
1972 — "Bloody Sunday": 13 protesters killed by troops in Derry
1973 — Last American soldiers leave Vietnam
1982 — 30,000 women circle perimeter of Greenham Common missile base
1984 — Miners' Strike in Britain: lasts for twelve months

DISCOGRAPHY

FOLK SONGS OF BRITAIN – Topic 12T 157-98
(A ten-volume collection of traditional singers recorded throughout Britain and Ireland)

Celtic lands
THE BAGPIPE – Lyrichord – LLST 7327
RENAISSANCE OF THE CELTIC HARP – ALAN STIVELL – Philips – 6414 406
CELTIC WEDDING – THE CHIEFTAINS – RCA – RL86358
A FEAST OF IRISH FOLK – Polydor – 2475 605
THE MIST COVERED MOUNTAIN – DE DANANN – Gael-linn – CEF087
THE BEST OF THE BOTHY BAND – Polydor – 2383 583
OPEN ROAD – BOYS OF THE LOUGH – Topic – 12T 5433
SCOTTISH TRADITION – BOTHY BALLADS – Tangent – TNGH109
SCOTTISH TRADITION – MUSIC FROM THE WESTERN ISLES – Tangent – TNGH 110
DOVE ACROSS THE WATER – OSSIAN – Iona – IR004

England
A SONG FOR EVERY SEASON – THE COPPER FAMILY – Leader – LEAB 404
FROST AND FIRE – THE WATERSONS – Topic – 12T 136
A GARLAND FOR SAM – SAM LARNER – Topic – 12T 244
THE MANCHESTER ANGEL – EWAN MACCOLL – Topic – 12T 147
OUT OF THE CUT – MARTIN CARTHY – Topic – 12TS 426
THAT LANCASHIRE BAND – THE OLDHAM TINKERS – Topic – 12TS 399
AMARANTH – SHIRLEY COLLINS – Harvest – SHSM 2008
LEIGE AND LIEF – FAIRPORT CONVENTION – Island – ILPS 9115
MORRIS ON – THE ALBION BAND – Island – IRSP 6

The United States
ANTHOLOGY OF AMERICAN FOLK MUSIC (three volumes) – Folkways – FA 2951-3
FOLK MUSIC IN AMERICA (fifteen volumes) – Library of Congress – LBC 1-15
POOR BOY – WOODY GUTHRIE – Transatlantic – TRS 113

Eastern Europe
FOLK MUSIC OF GREECE – Topic – 12TS 231
THE MUSIC OF BULGARIA – Hannibal – HNBL 1335
FOLK MUSIC OF ALBANIA – Topic – 12T 154
STREETS OF GOLD – THE KLEZMORIM – Arhoolie – 3011

COLLECTIONS OF FOLK SONGS

Folk Songs Collected by Ralph Vaughan Williams, ed. Roy Palmer
(J.M. Dent, 1983 – ISBN 0 460 04558 X)

Everyman's Book of British Ballads, ed. Roy Palmer
(J.M. Dent, 1980 – ISBN 0 460 04452 4)

Everyman's Book of English Country Songs, ed. Roy Palmer
(J.M. Dent, 1979 – ISBN 0 460 12048 4)

The English Folksinger, ed. Sam Richards and Trish Stubbs
(Collins, 1979 – ISBN 000 411 068 4)

Traveller's Songs from England and Scotland, ed. Ewan MacColl and Peggy Seeger
(Routledge and Kegan Paul, 1977 – ISBN 0 7100 8436 6)

Canu'r Cymru, a collection of Welsh folk songs edited by Phyllis Kinney and Meredydd
Evans (Welsh Folk-Song Society, 1987 – ISBN 0 900426 58 6)

American Ballads and Folk Songs, collected by John and Alan Lomax
(MacMillan, New York, 1934)

INDEX